Liz Wants a Dog

Written by Kassi Gilmour

Practise the sounds

a b c d e f g h i j k l m n
o p qu r s t u v w x y z
ck wh ll ss ff zz th sh ch ng
oo oo th ai ee oa or er

Practise blending sounds

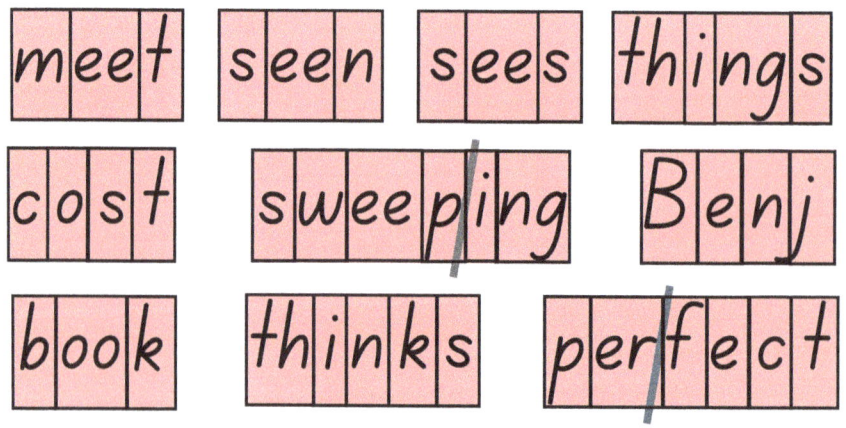

Practise tricky words

said what want <u>want</u>s saw be <u>be</u>gins
were one some come little here there
where so put very down out <u>about</u>

Liz Wants a Dog

Set 6

Written by Kassi Gilmour

Little Liz wants a dog.

She thinks dogs are the best.

"Mum, can I have a dog?" she begs.

"No Liz, I have too much to do, and dogs need lots of things," Mum tells Liz.

Liz gets a book all about dogs. She longs for one.

"Mum, if I help, can I have a dog?" Liz begs.

Mum was sweeping and said,
"No Liz, dogs cost too much."

Liz pats all the dogs she sees.
She likes dogs very much.

Mum tells her pal, Hez, that Liz wants a dog.

Hez begins to look for a pup.

One day, Hez rings to tell Mum she has seen the perfect dog.

The next day, they all go to meet Benj.

Mum said yes!

Questions:

1. What does Liz want?
2. Why does she want a dog?
3. Why did Mum say no?
4. How did Liz show that she loved dogs?
5. Why do you think Mum changed her mind?

Liz and Benj

Written by Kassi Gilmour

Practise the sounds

u l ll ss ff b j w wh y
th sh v qu z zz x
ch ng oo oo th
ai ee oa or er

Practise blending sounds

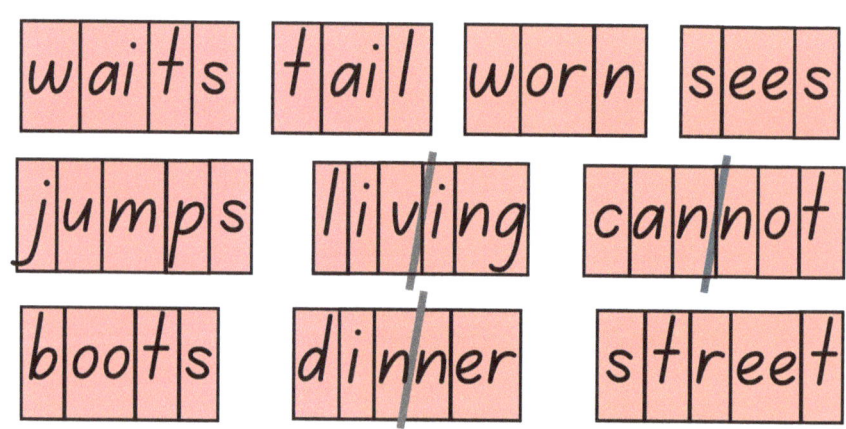

Practise tricky words

said what want saw be <u>a</u>long
were one some come little here there
where so <u>pu</u>ts very down out

Liz and Benj

Set 6

WRITTEN BY KASSI GILMOUR

Little Benj cannot wait for Liz to get back.

He waits all day long.

His tail is still, and he rests.

When he sees Liz get back, he jumps up.

Benj wags his tail and yaps.

He runs to Liz.

Liz skips to the living room and sits down.

Benj jumps up for a hug and a pat. He likes long hugs.

Then, Liz and Benj have dinner.

Next, Liz puts her boots on.
Benj yaps and wags his tail.
He is very glad.

They go for a stroll along the street.

Benj looks and sniffs.

He runs and pants.

Liz picks up his poo and puts it in a bin.

When they get back from a good, long stroll, Benj is worn out.

He will sleep well.

Questions:

1. Why does Benj wait by the window all day?
2. What happens when Benj sees Liz drive home?
3. Tell me three things Liz and Benj do together?
4. Why is Benj tired?
5. Do you have a pet? If so, what do you do with your pet?

Gold Dust

Written by Kassi Gilmour

Practise the sounds

u l ll ss ff b j w wh y
th sh v qu z zz x
ch ng oo oo th
ai ee oa or er

Practise blending sounds

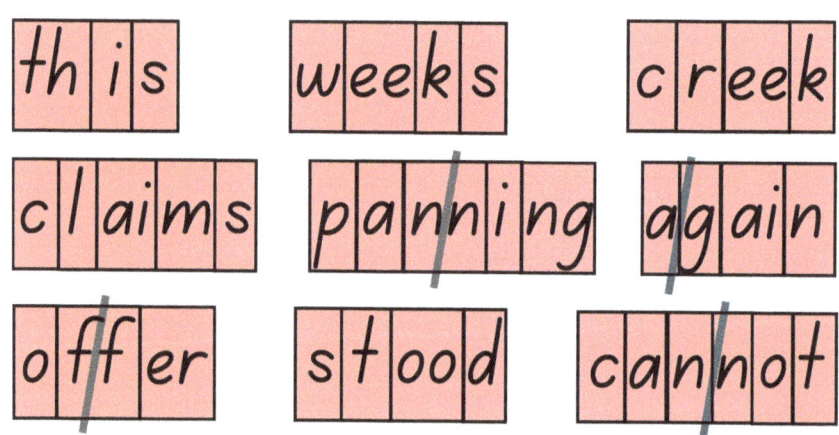

Practise tricky words

a go ago said what want saw be were one some come little here there where so put very down out <u>about</u>

Gold Dust

Set 6

Written by Kassi Gilmour

"Long ago, there was gold in this creek," Pop said.

He told me all about the old days, when he spent weeks panning for gold.

Pop took an old pan and stood in the creek.

He bent down and dug the pan into the sand and rocks.

He shook the pan, and took the big rocks out.

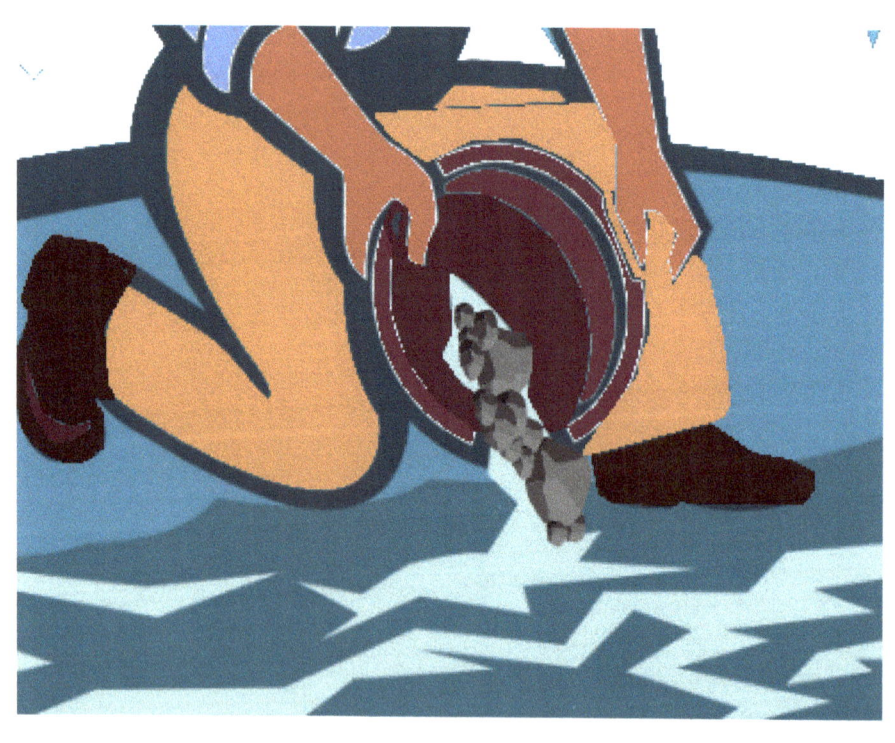

Pop took a very good look in the pan.

There was no gold in the pan.

So, Pop took a step to the left, and put his pan back into the creek.

He dug his pan into the sand and rocks again.

Pop took a long look in the pan. He saw a speck of gold. He told me that it was gold dust.

"You cannot get rich with gold dust," he claims.

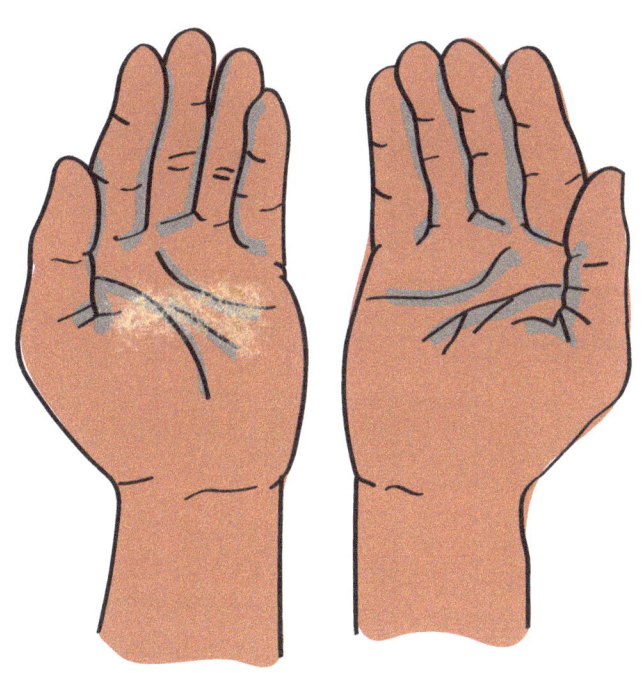

I offer to help Pop.

I want some gold, too.

Questions:

1. What did Pop do when he was younger?
2. How does Pop pan for gold?
3. Does he find gold?
4. Will the gold dust make Pop rich?
5. Why do you think the boy wants to pan for gold?

Oliver

Written by Kassi Gilmour

Practise the sounds

u l ll ss ff b j w wh y
th sh v qu z zz x
ch ng oo oo th
ai ee oa or er

Practise blending sounds

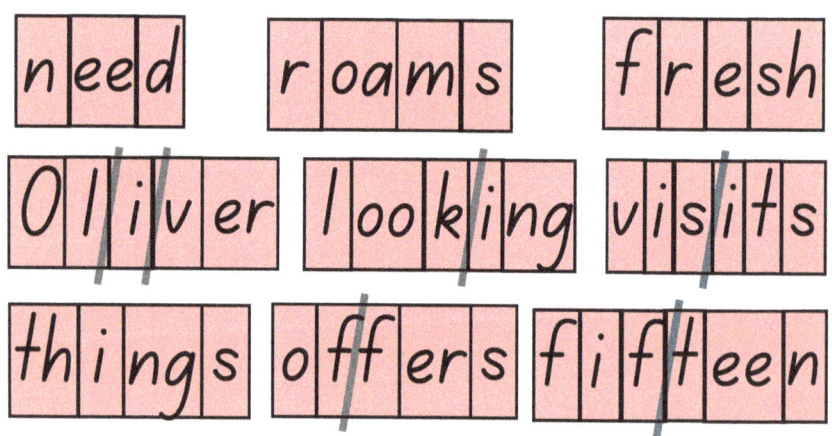

Practise tricky words

said what <u>want</u>s saw be were one
some come little here there where so
<u>pu</u>ts very down out <u>about</u> <u>out</u>fit

Oliver

Set 6

Written by Kassi Gilmour

Oliver is fifteen.

There are lots of things that Oliver wants to get.

"I need some cash," he told his mum.

Oliver's mum said, "If you want some cash, you will need to get a job."

Oliver thinks this is a good plan.

He puts on a fresh outfit to look for a job.

Oliver visits a shop and chats with the boss.

He roams from shop to shop, looking for a job.

When Oliver gets back, he tells his mum all about his day.

The next day, Oliver gets a call from one of the shops. The boss offers him a job.

Oliver likes his job and he is good at it.

Best of all, Oliver has some cash to get some of the things he wants.

Questions:

1. Why does Oliver want money?
2. What does his mum tell him to do, if he wants money?
3. Why does Oliver change his clothes?
4. Who does Oliver talk to at the shop?
5. Do you think Oliver is happy to have a job? Why?